Artist Swears

Vulgar Word Coloring Book
To Rant & Relax

By

S.B. Nozaz

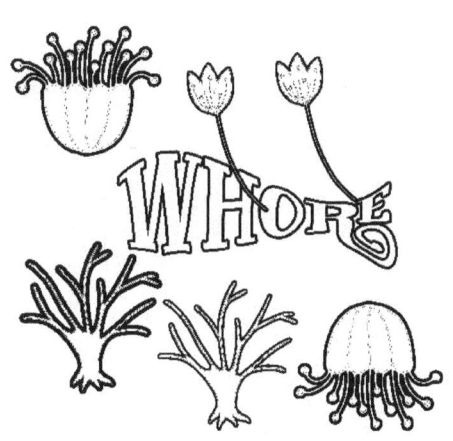

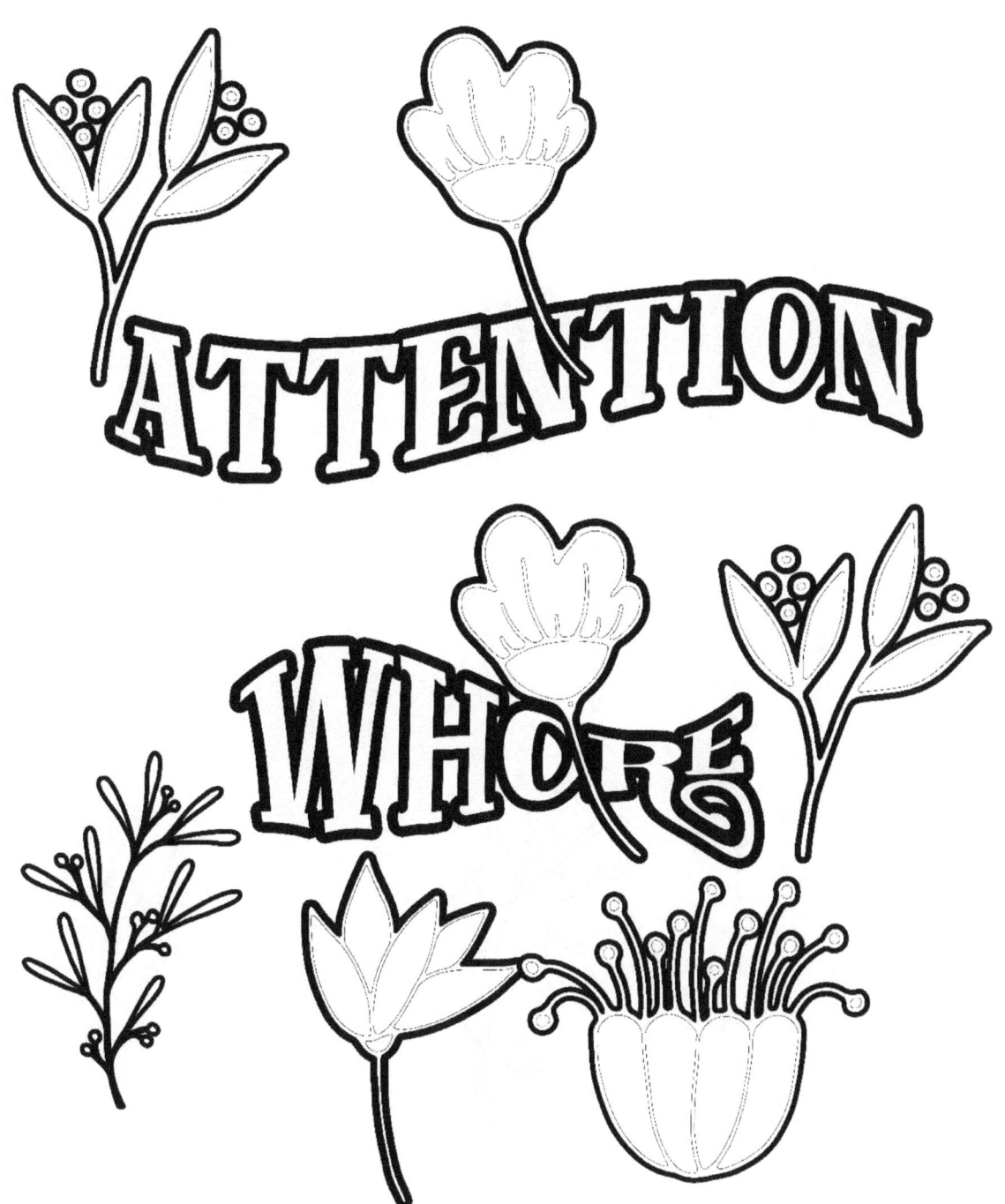

FUCK A DUCK

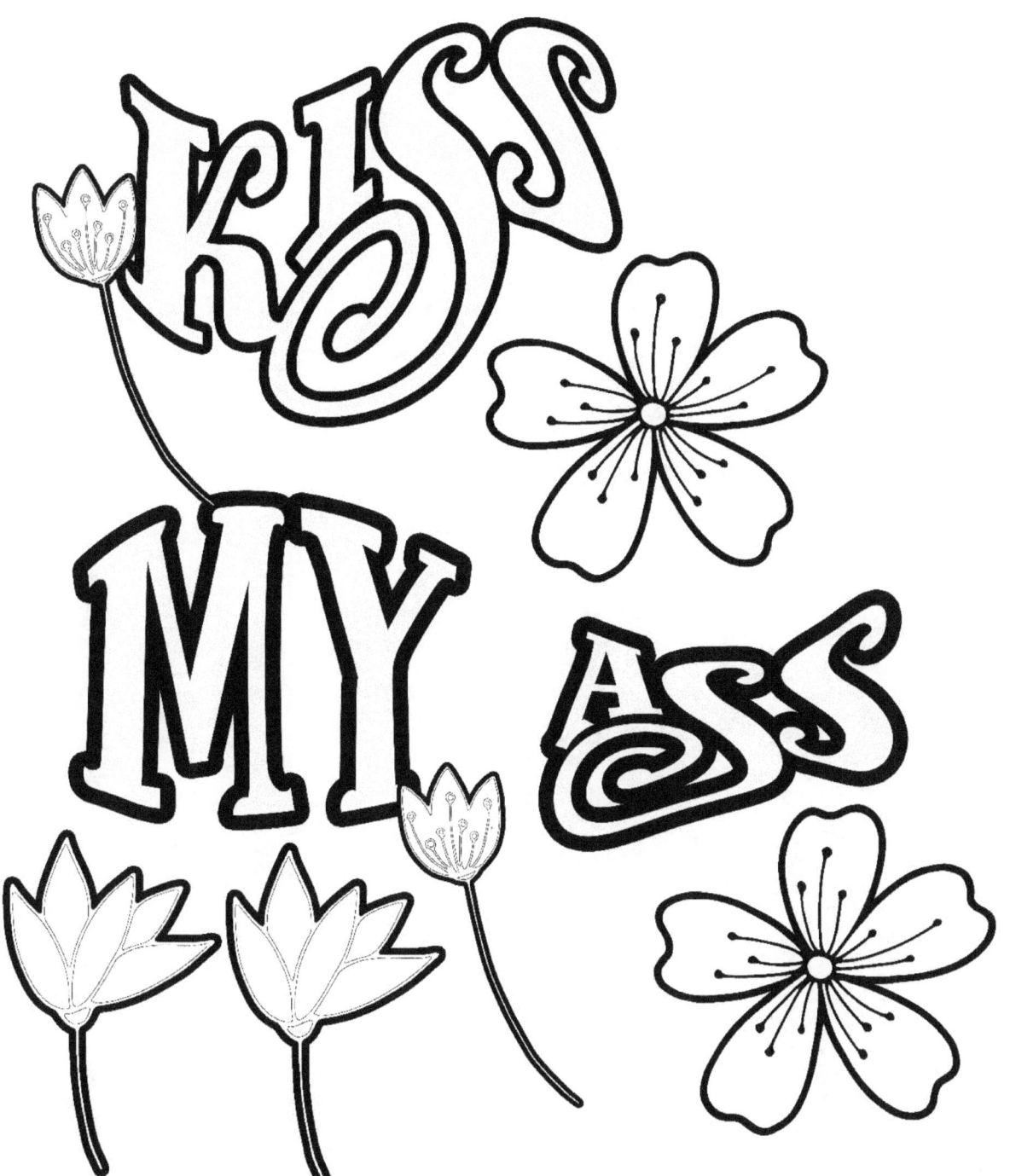

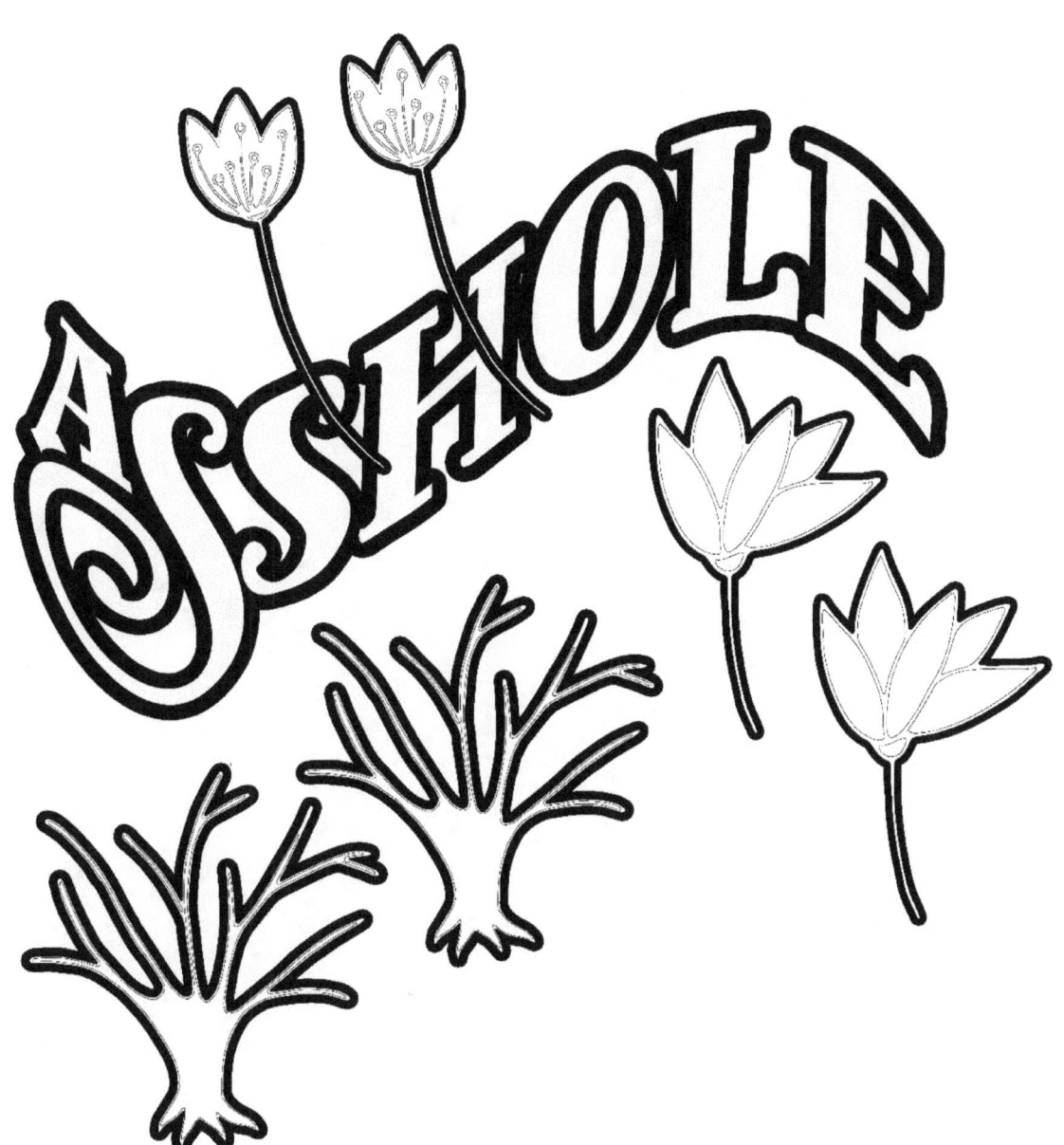

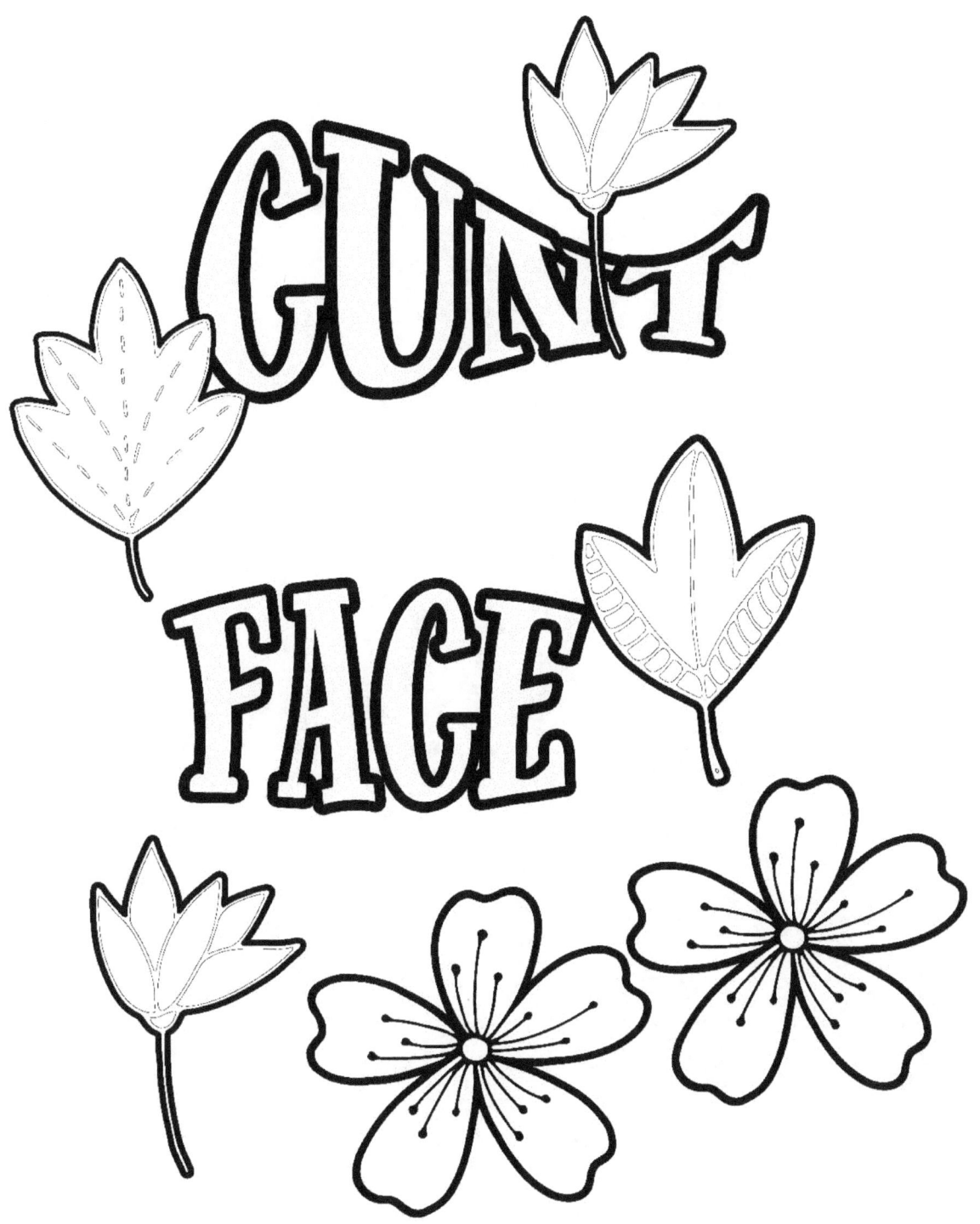

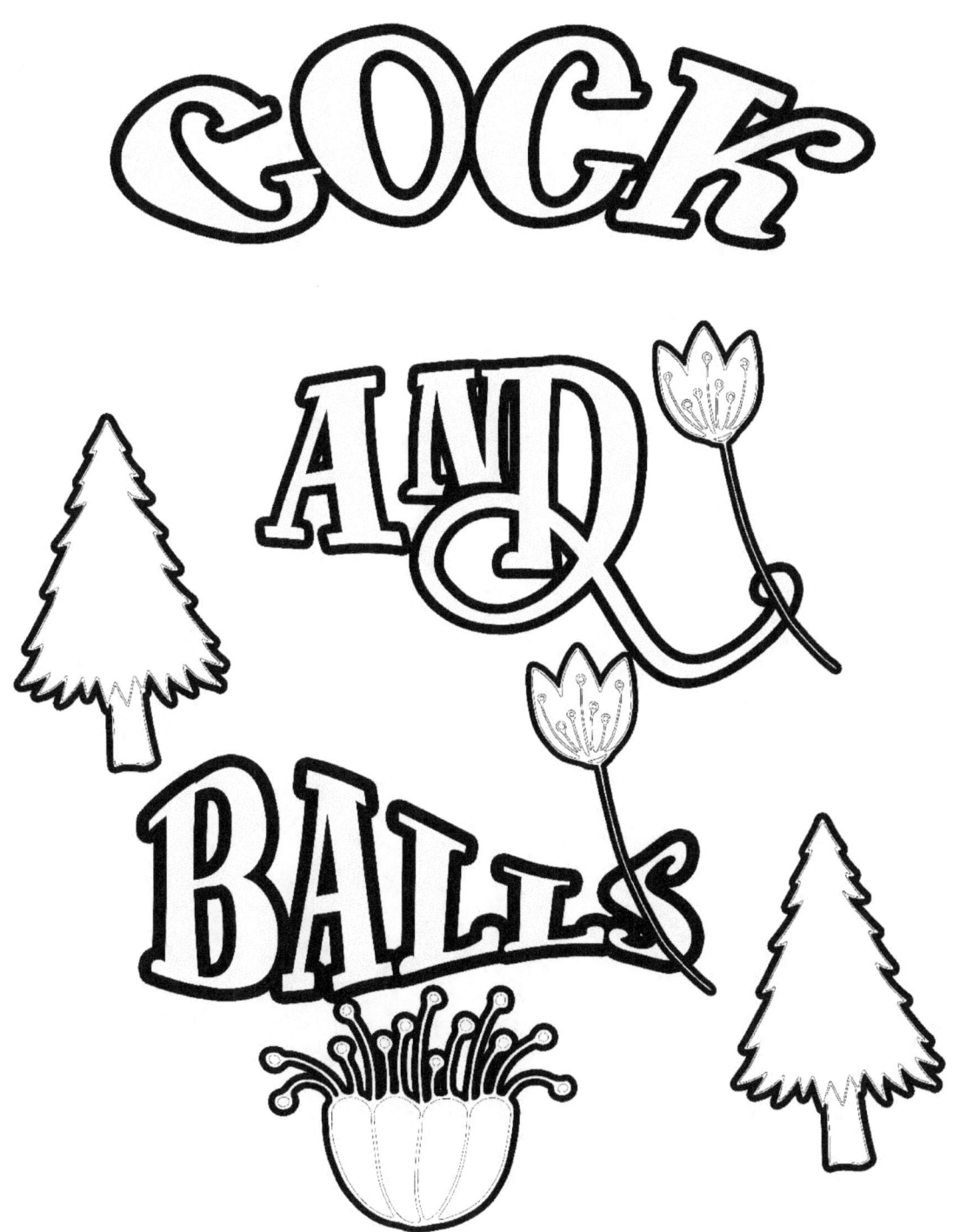

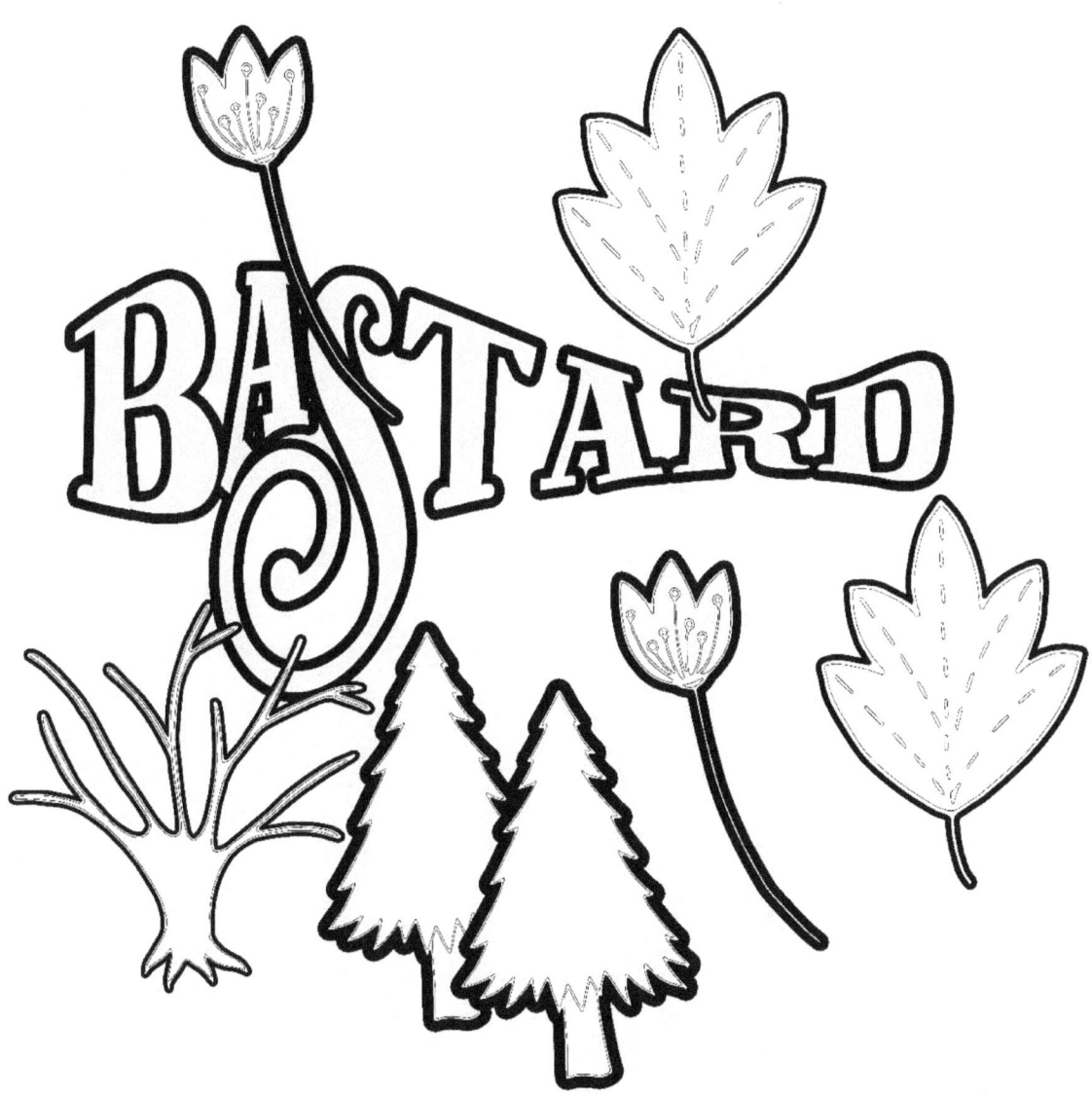

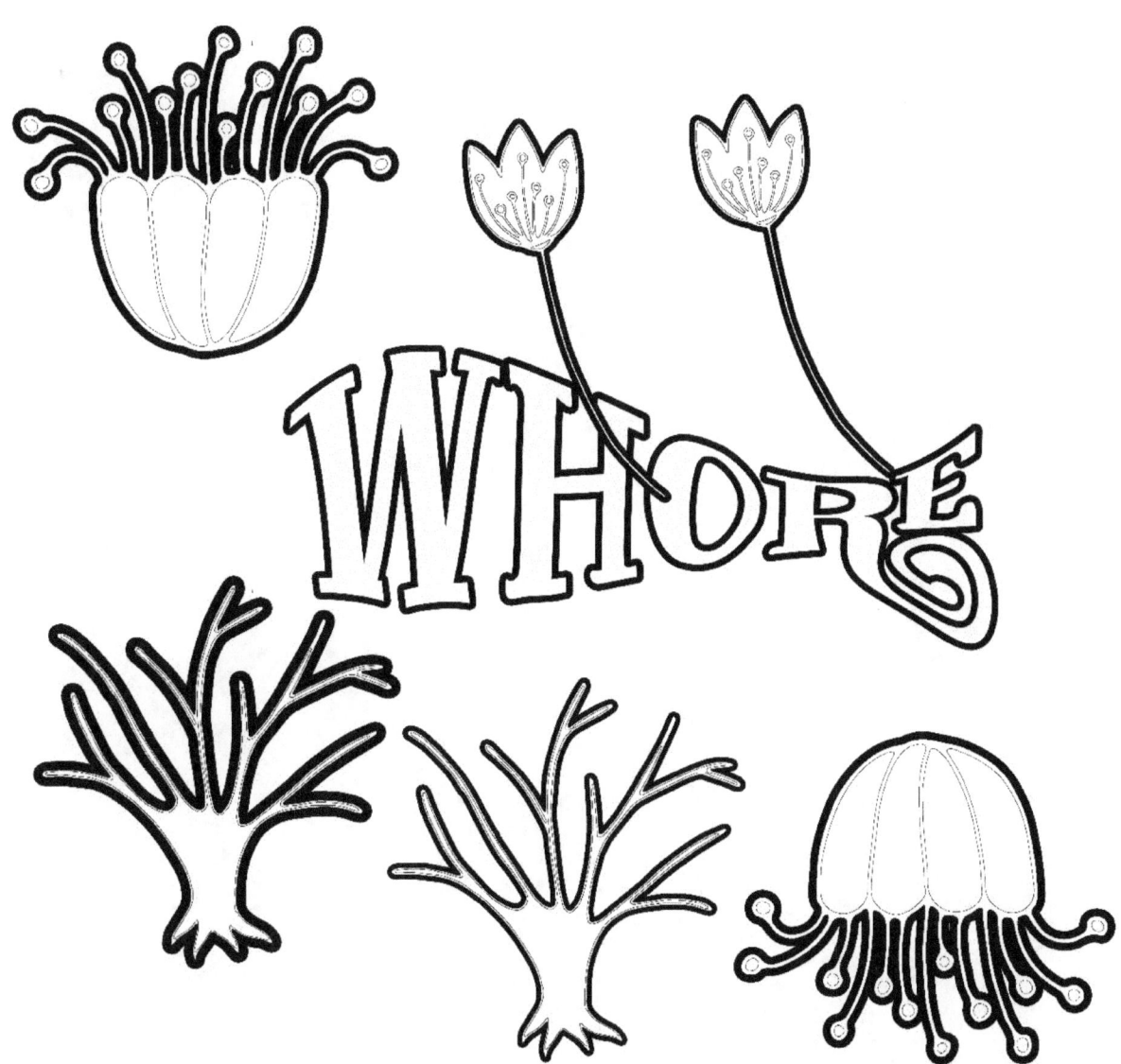

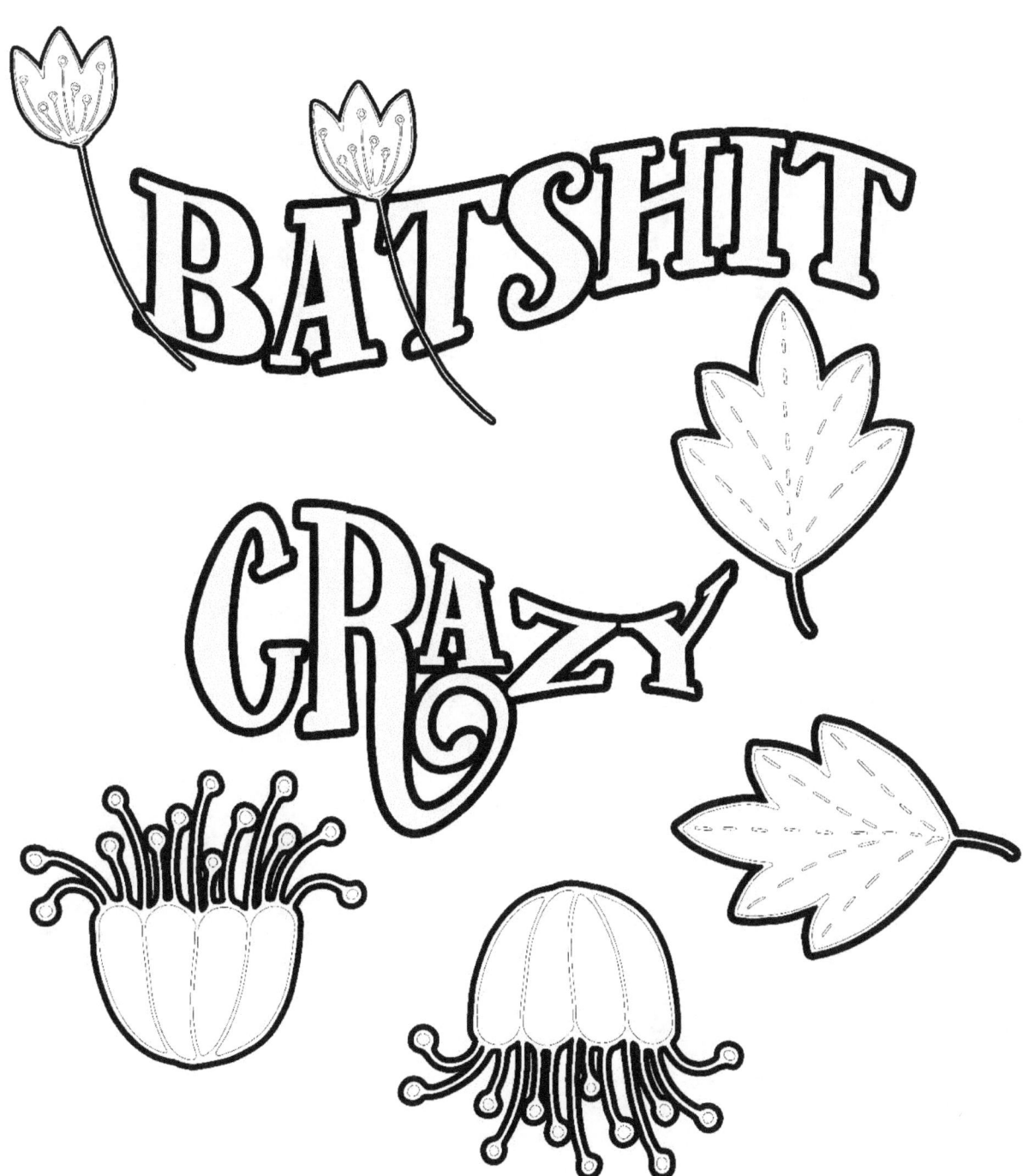

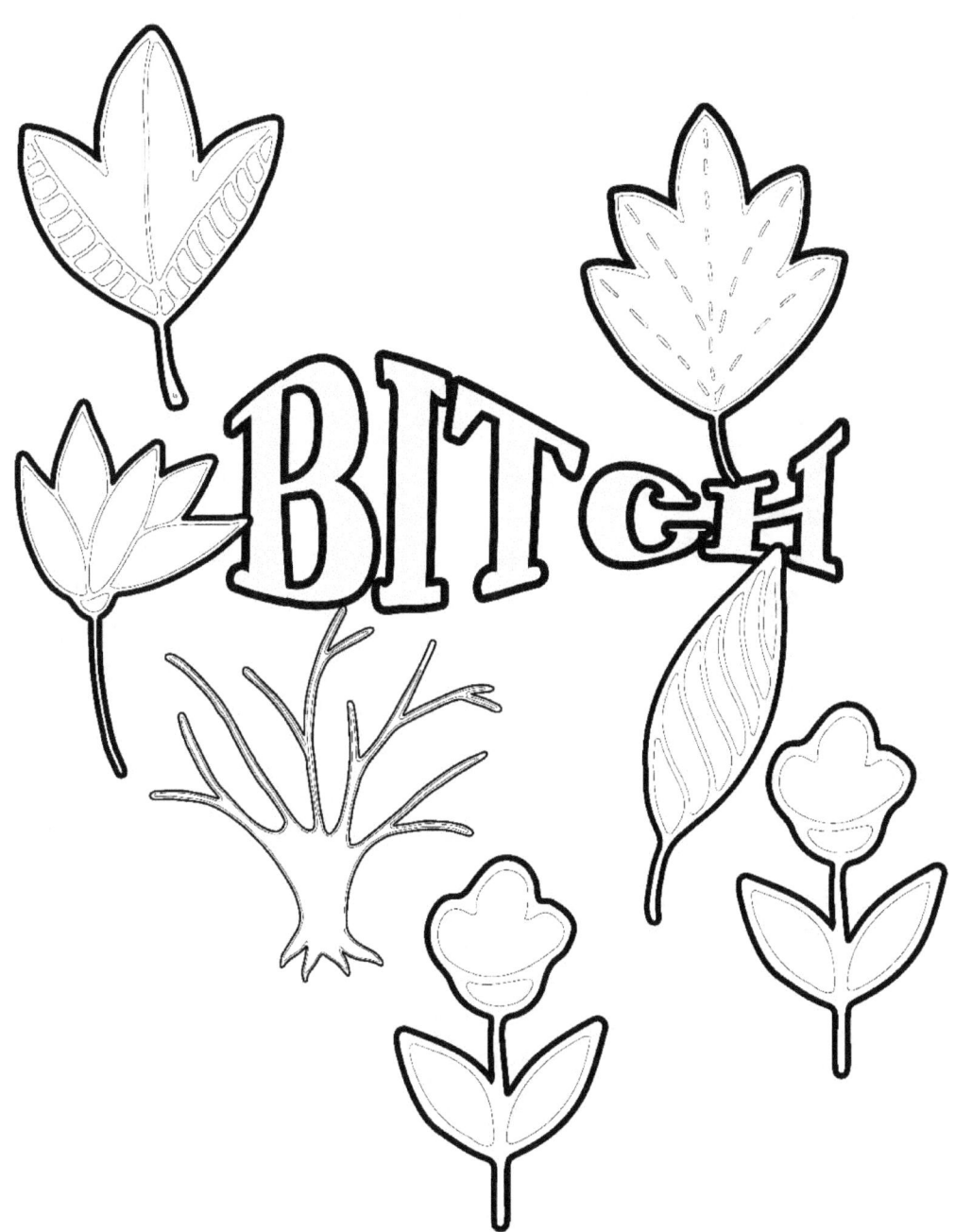

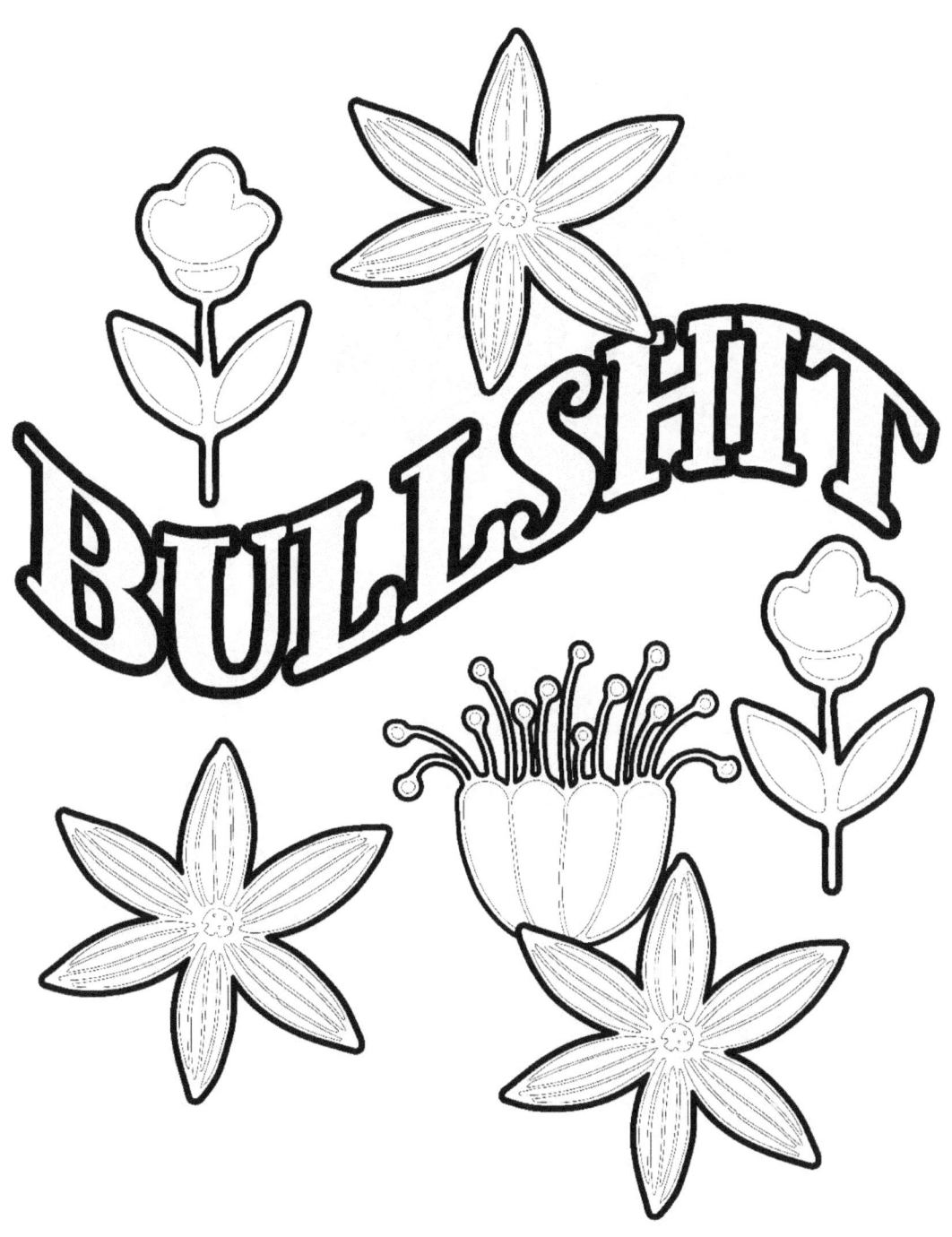

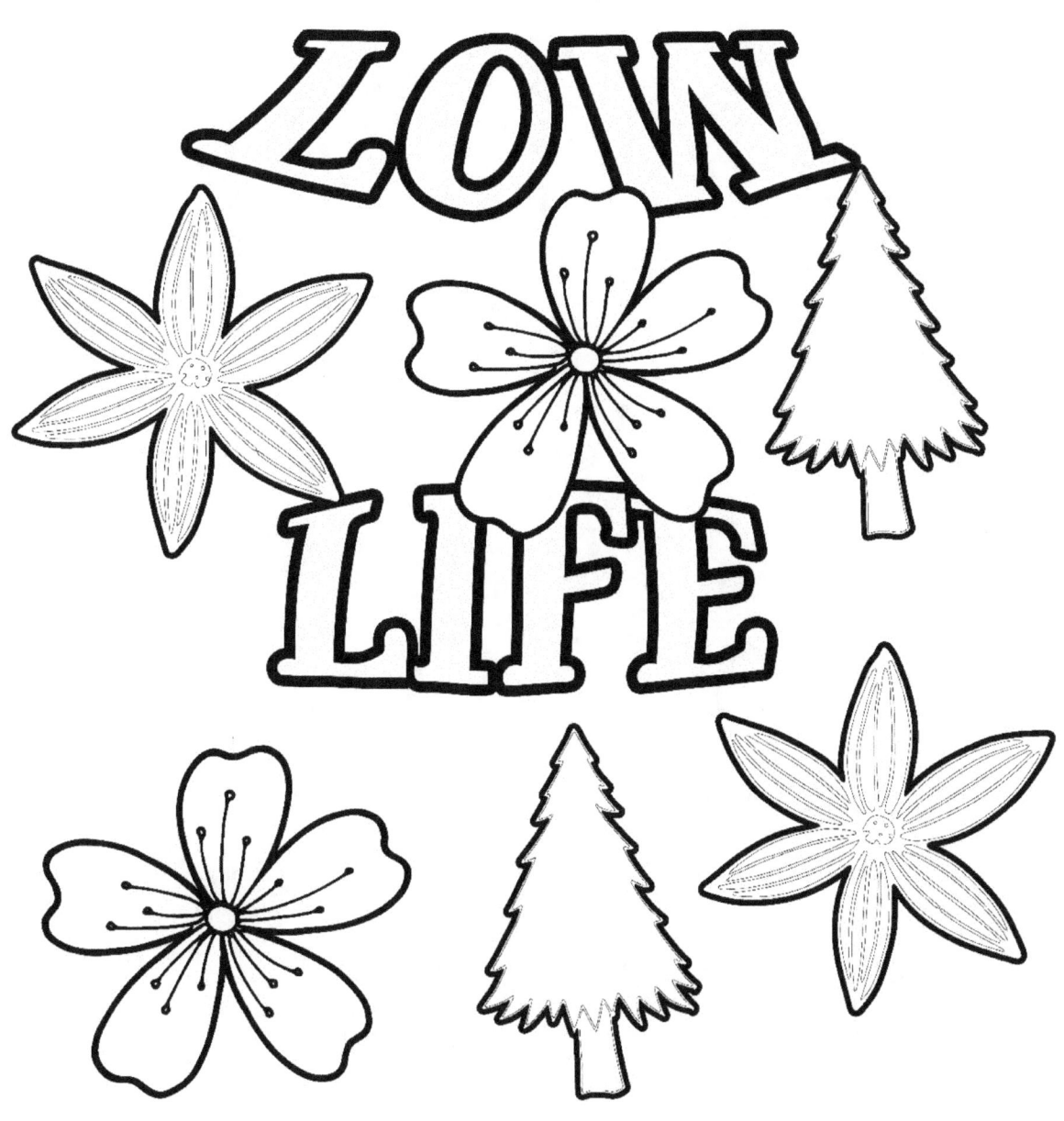

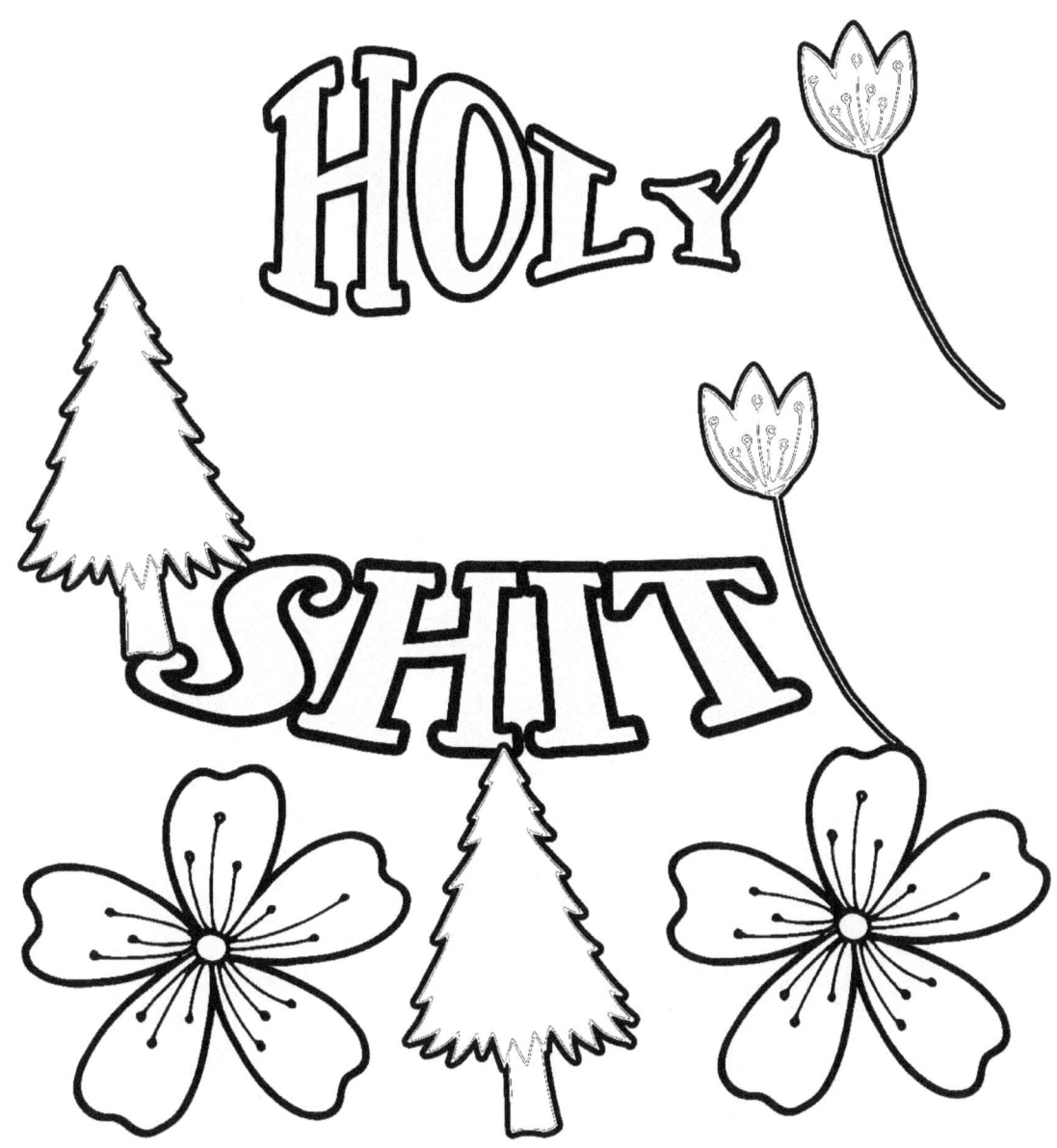

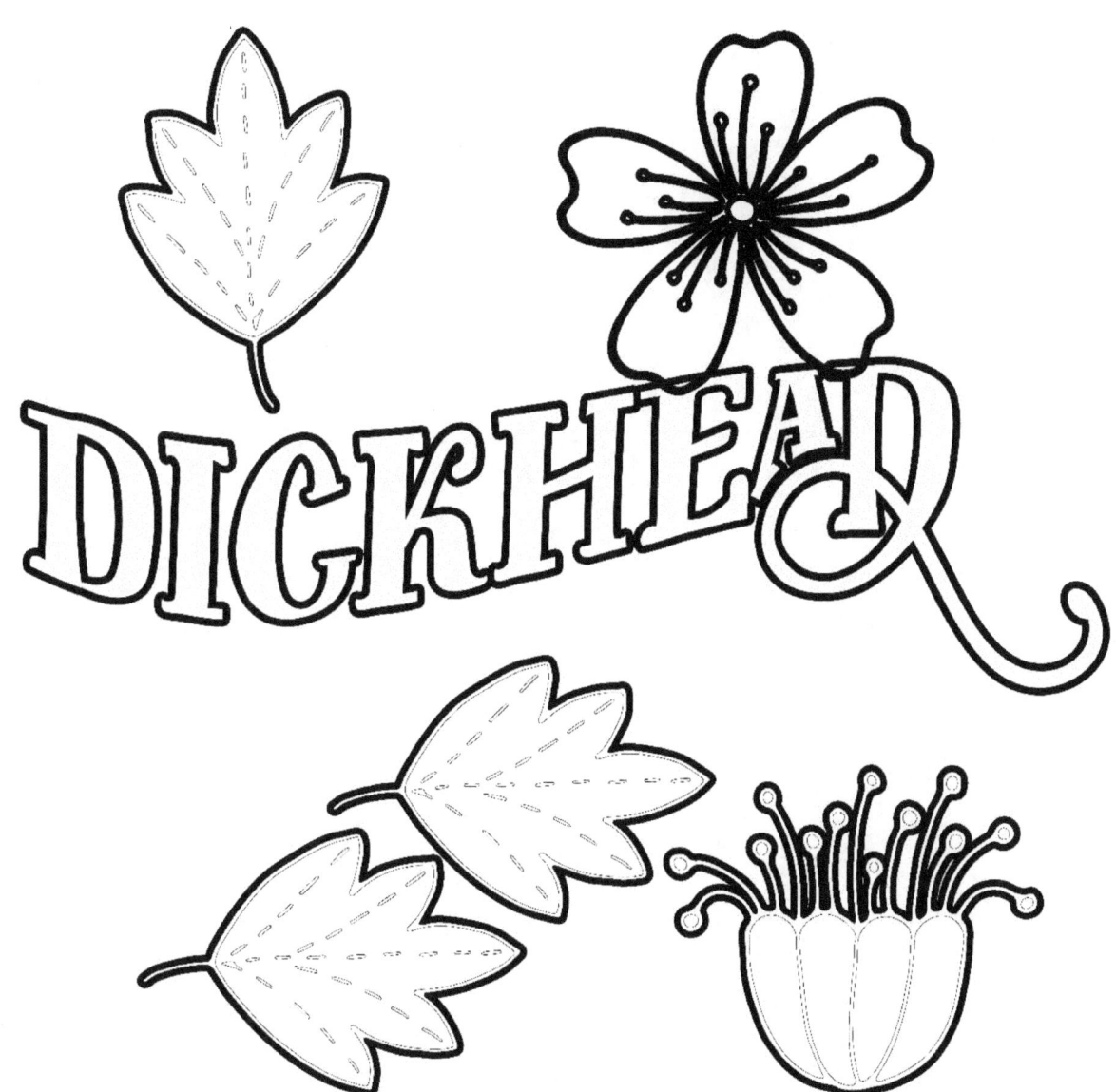

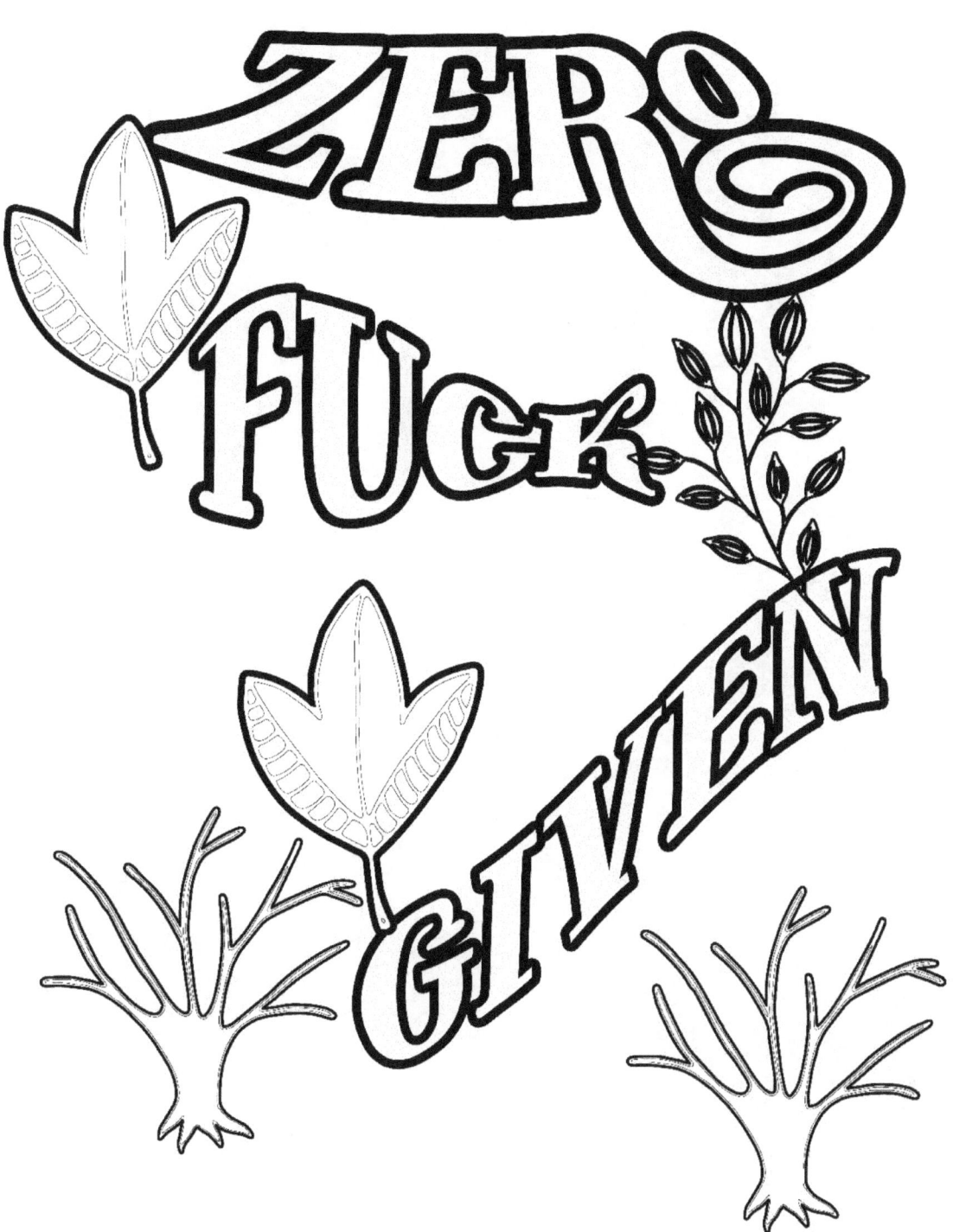

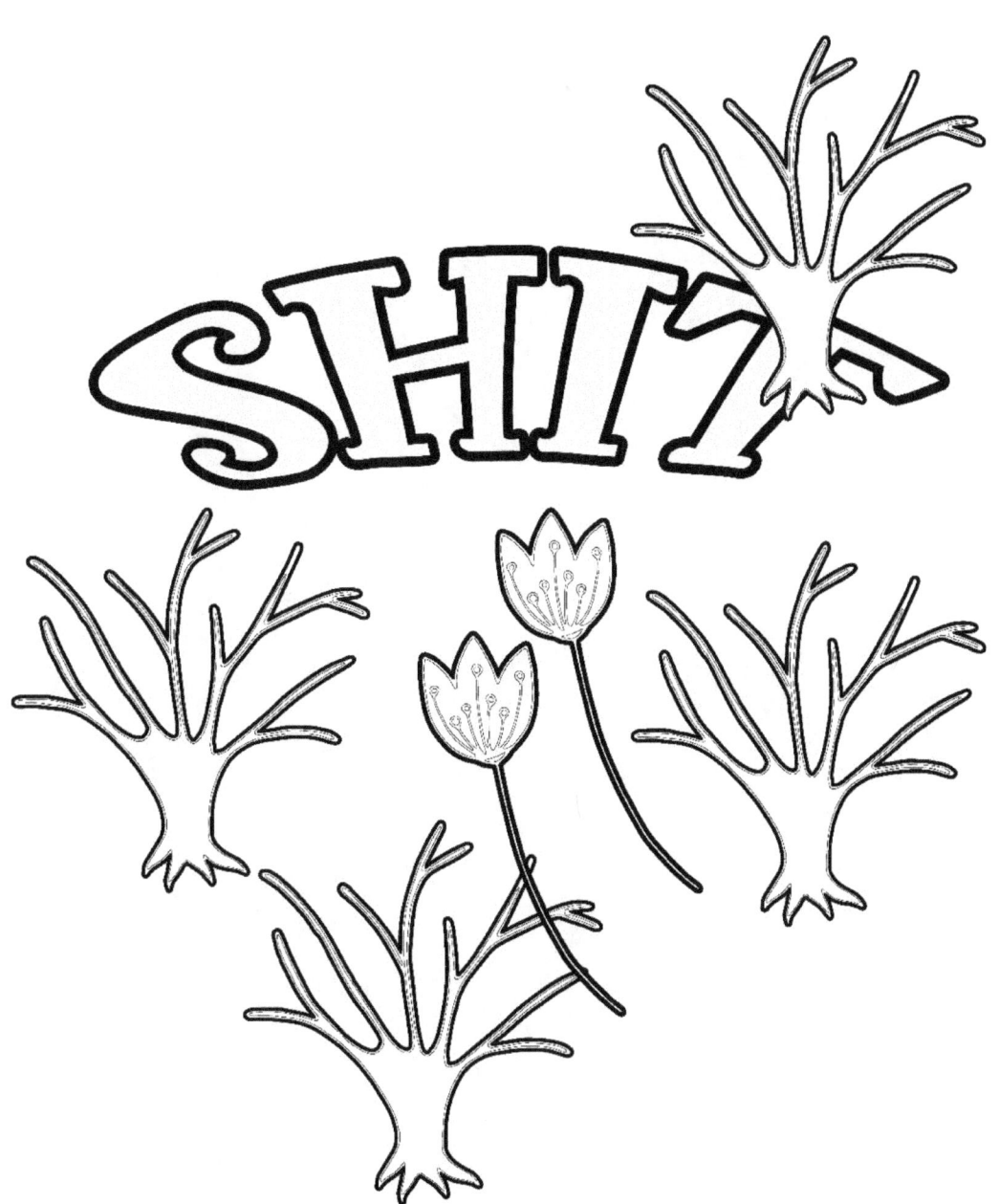

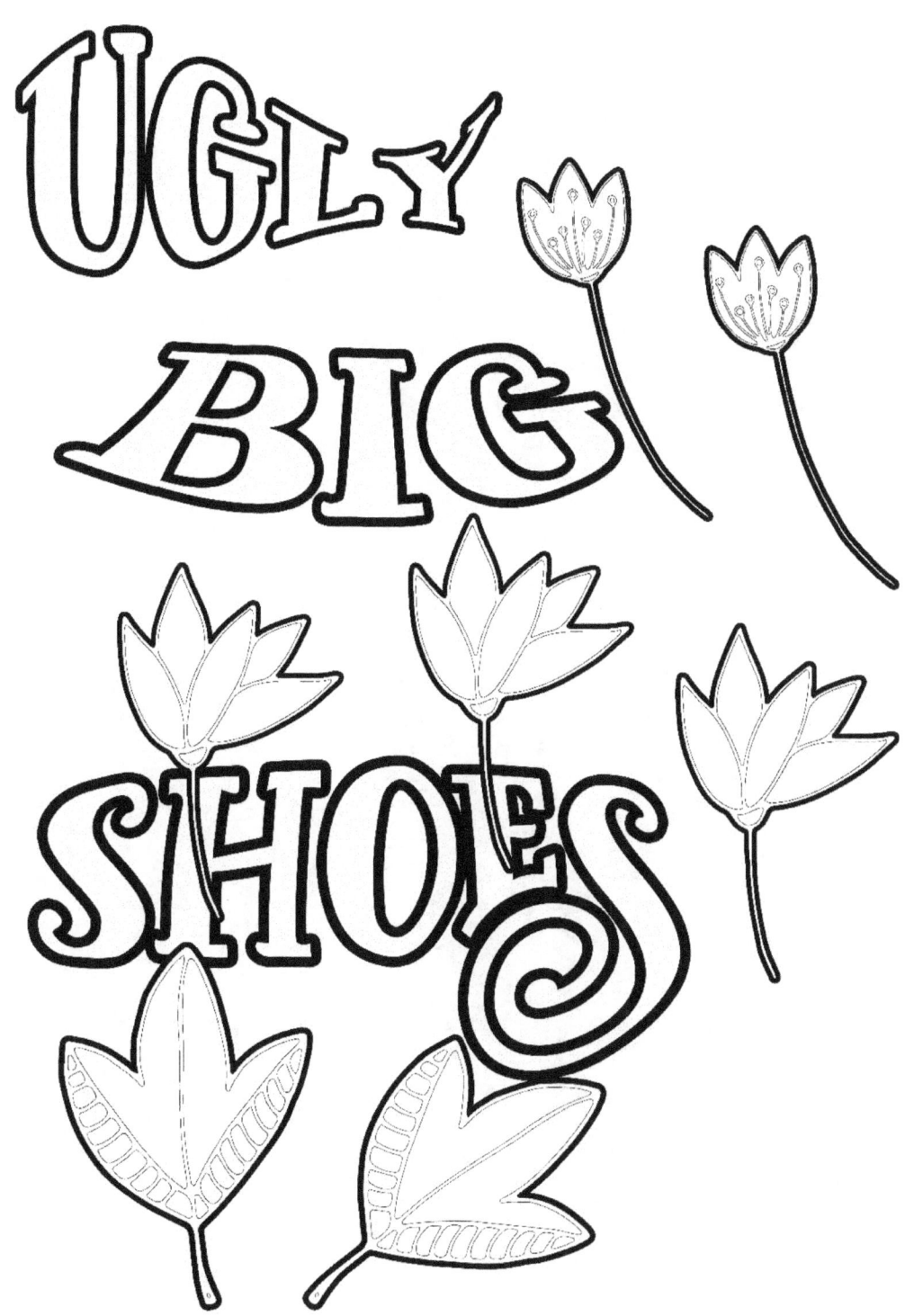

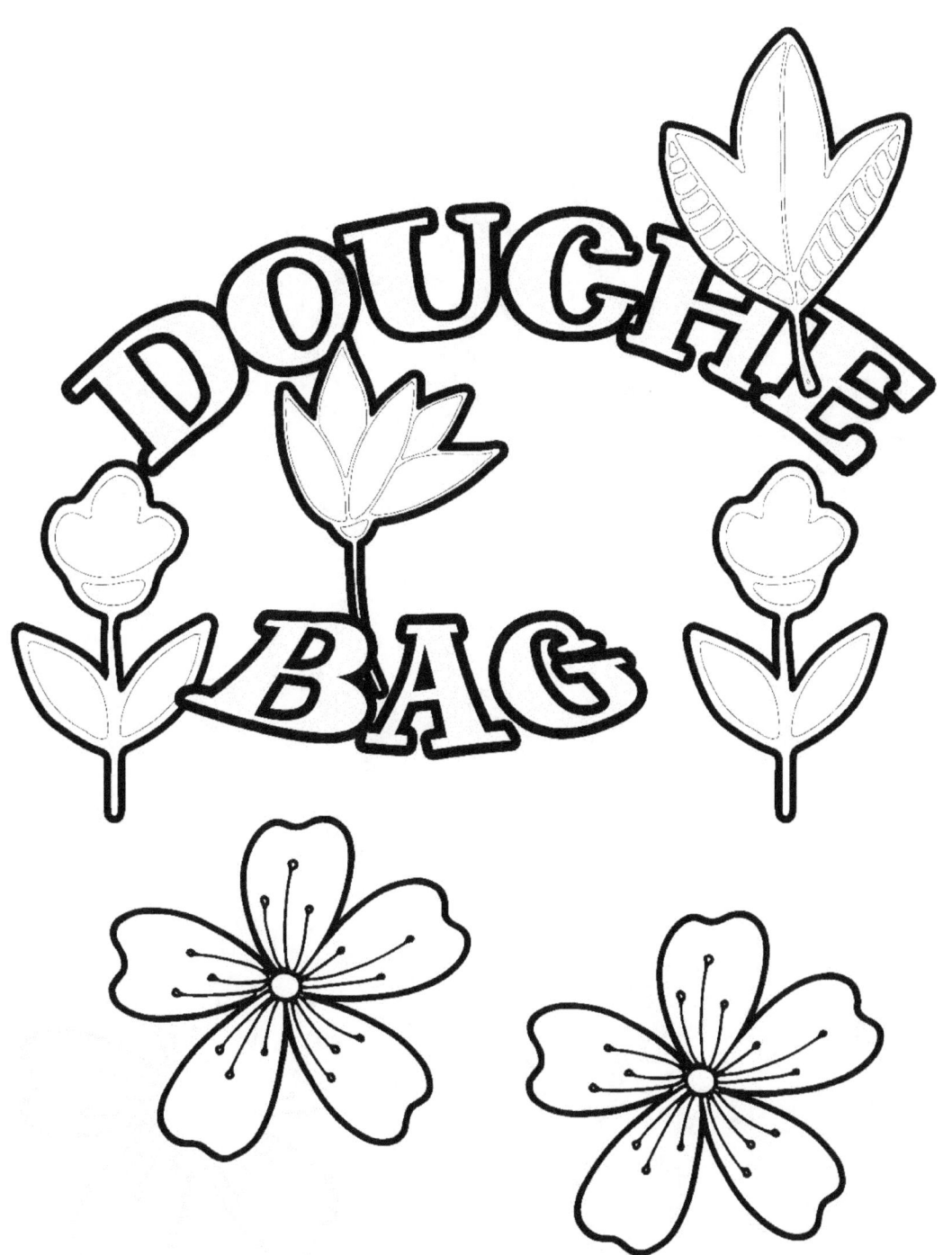

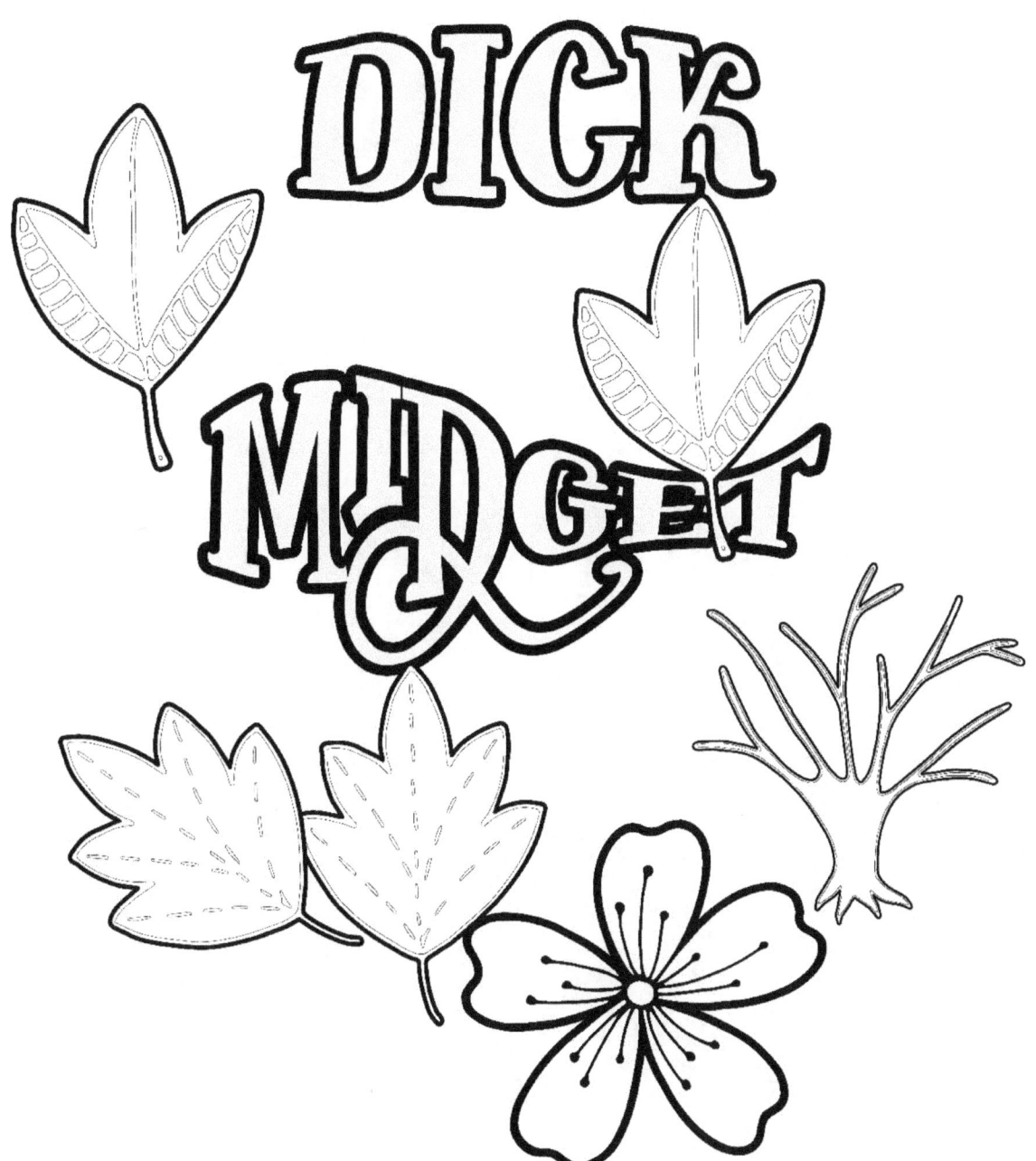

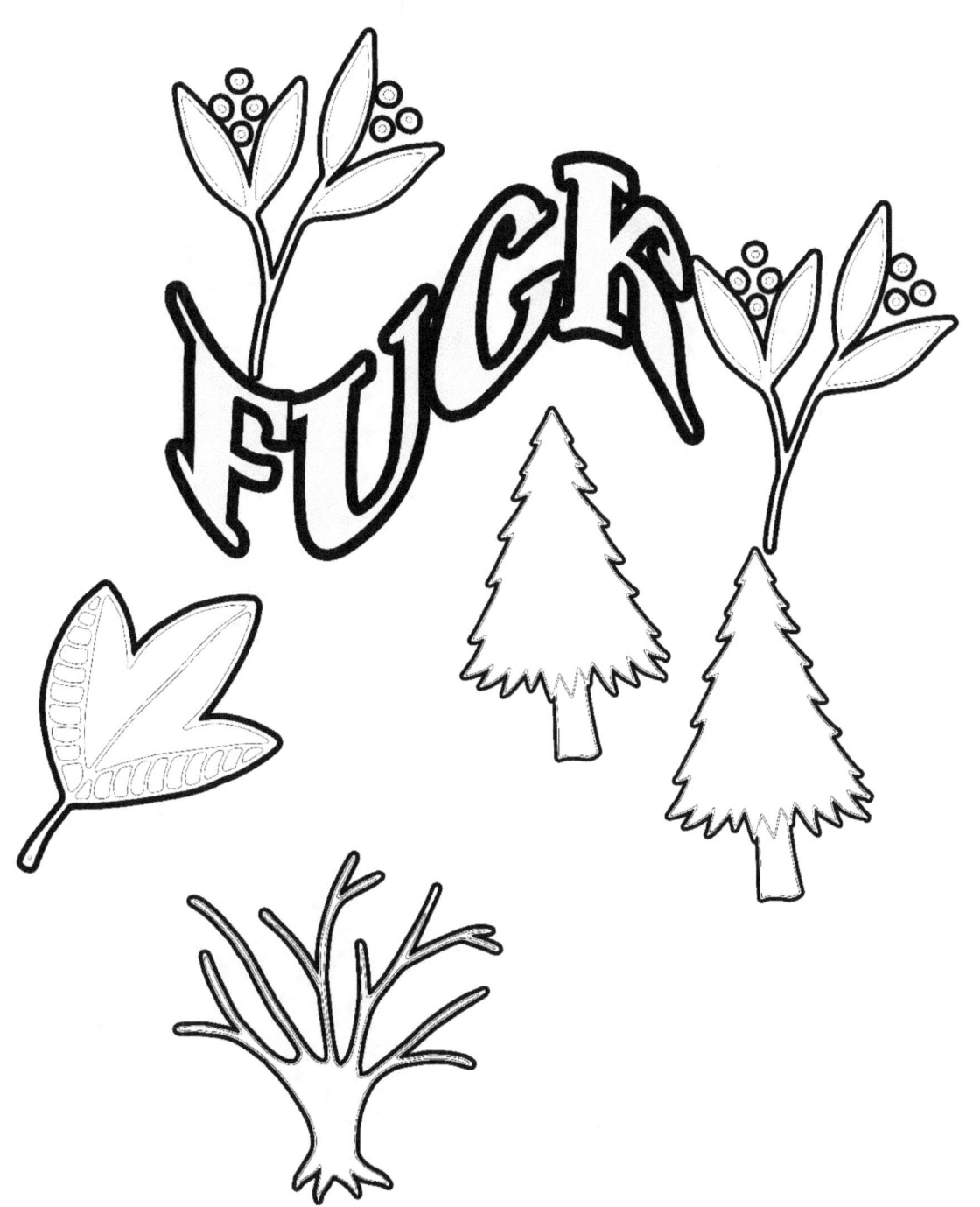

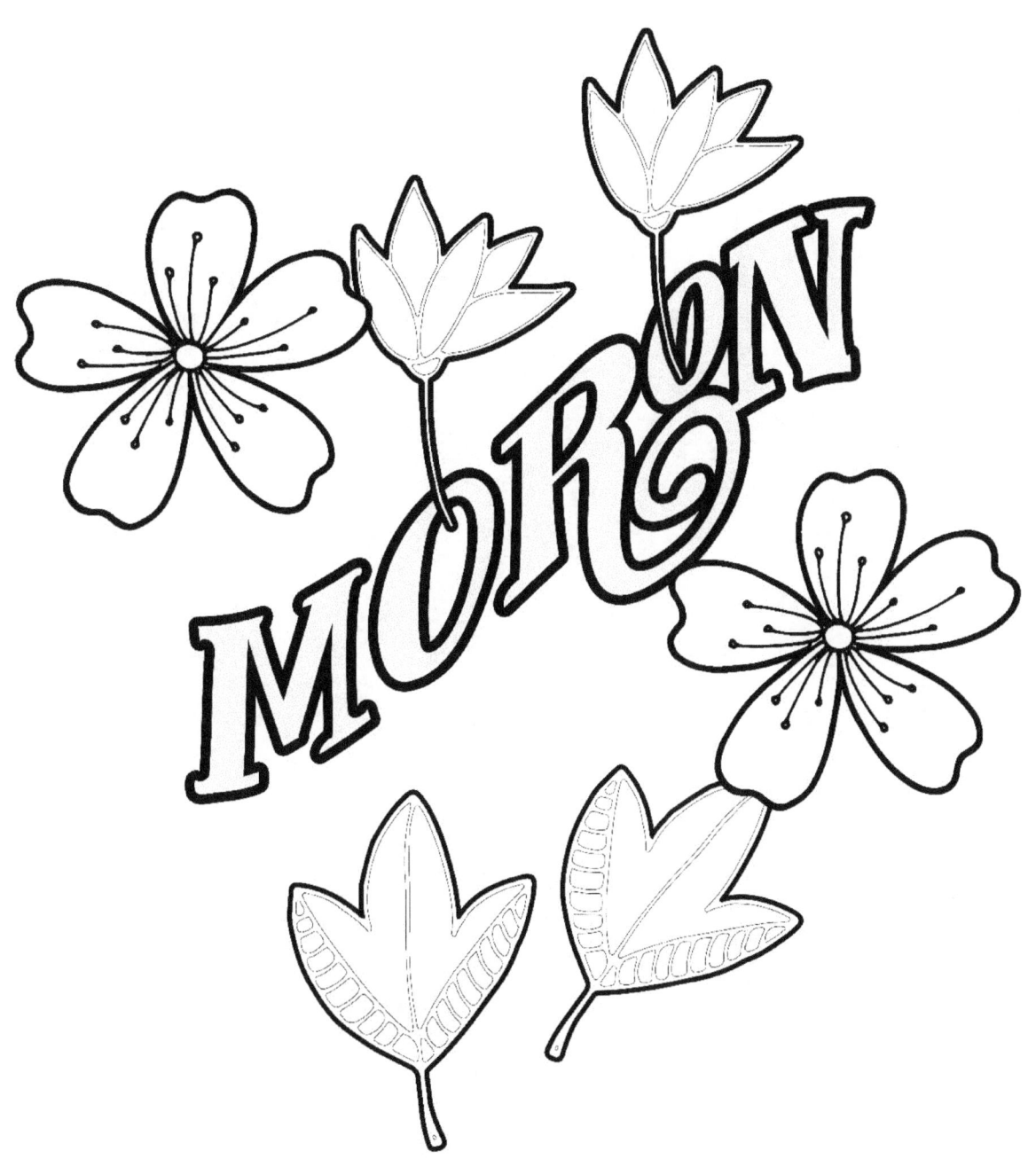

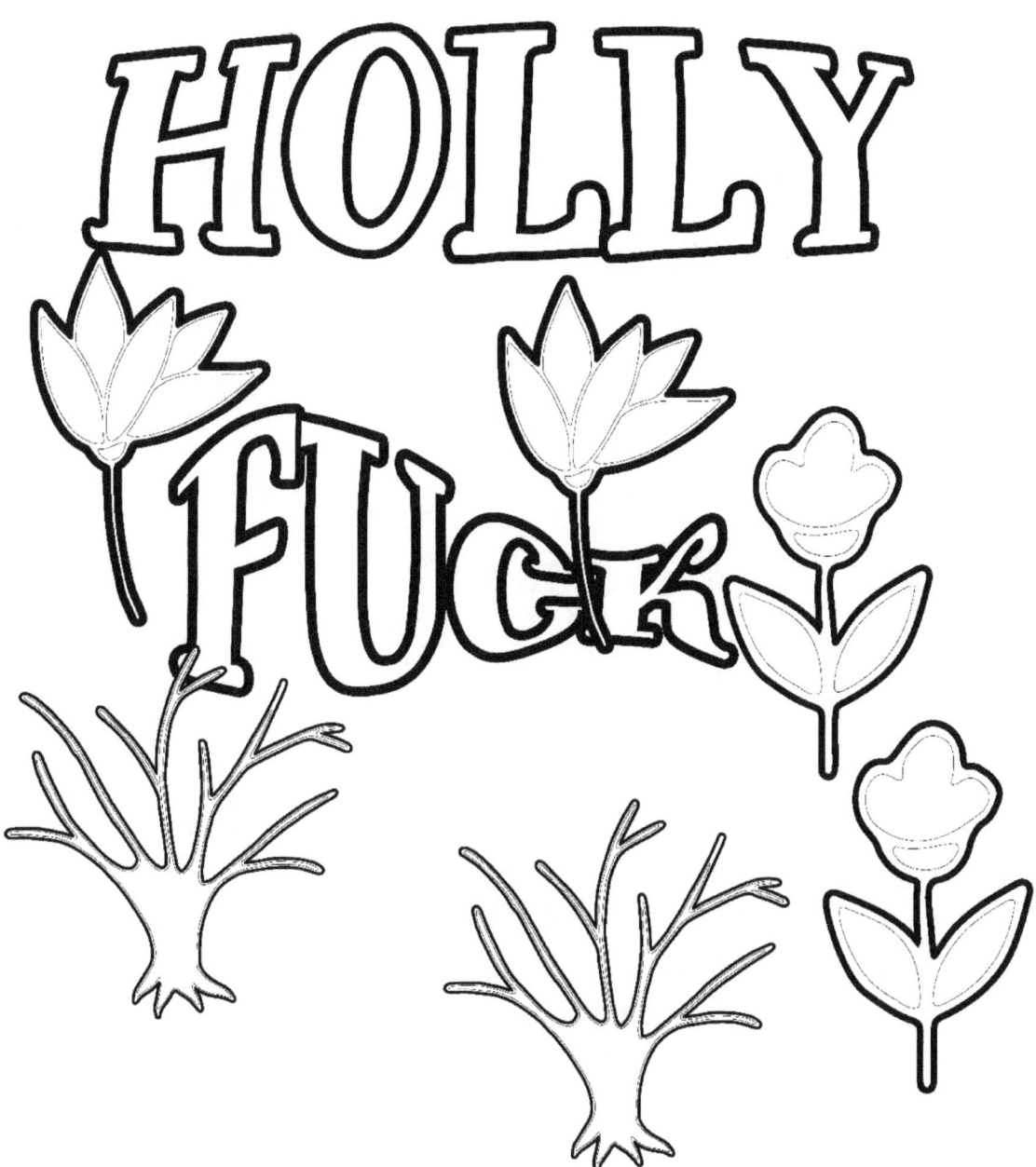

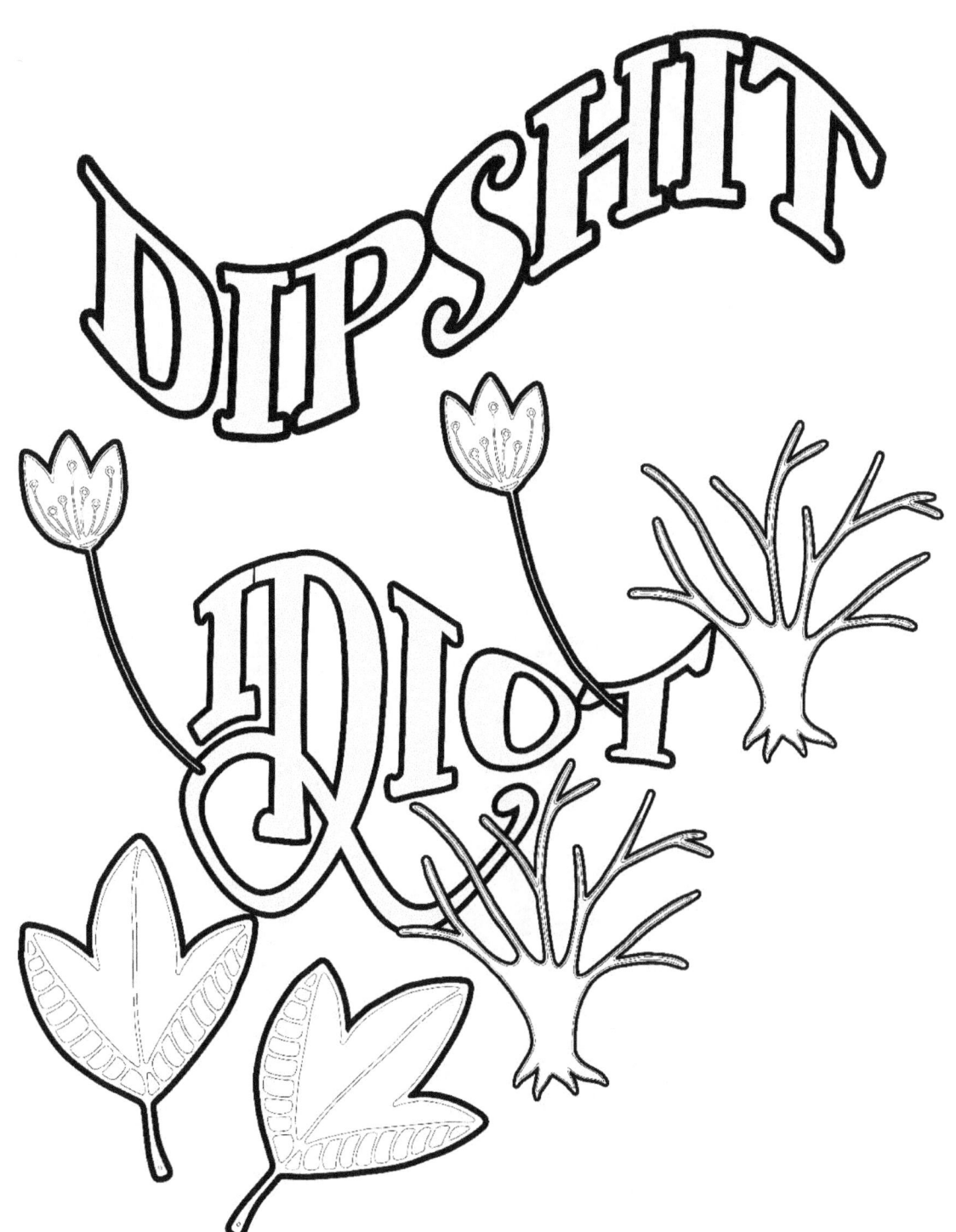

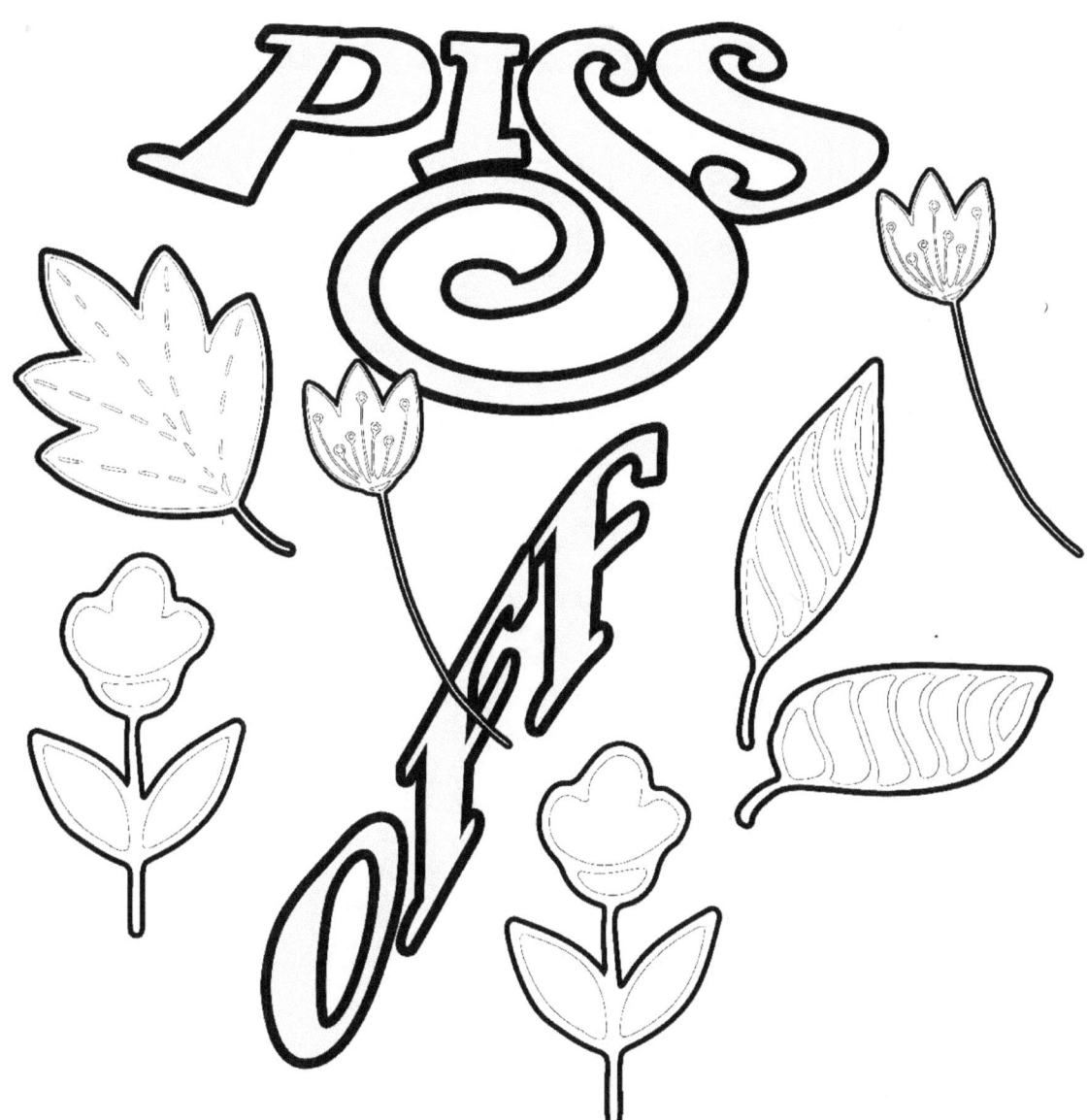

Note

www.ingramcontent.com/pod-product-compliance
Lightning Source LLC
Chambersburg PA
CBHW080636190526
45169CB00009B/3415